Poems 4 A.M.

Poems 4 A.M.

Susan Minot

ALFRED A. KNOPF

NEW YORK

2003

The author would like to thank Deborah Garrison,
who was so helpful in putting together these poems.

THIS IS A BORZOI BOOK
PUBLISHED BY ALFRED A. KNOPF

"St. Sebastian in Your Kitchen" was previously published in *Rivercity*,
the University of Memphis, Memphis, Tennessee. "The Toast" was
previously published in *The New Yorker*.

Library of Congress Cataloging-in-Publication Data
Minot, Susan.
Poems 4 A.M. / by Susan Minot.—1st ed.
p.   cm.
ISBN 0-375-70955-X
1. Love poetry, American.   I. Title.
PS3563.I4755 P64 2002
811'.54—dc21
2001050501

Manufactured in the United States of America
Published May 15, 2002
First paperback edition, October 10, 2003

For sister Carrie,
longest friend

Contents

I. MASSACHUSETTS

Boston Ancestors

I hear them behind me
crossing Persian rugs on heel-less shoes,
drinking Dubonnet, eating nuts
(from the pantry the smell of stew),
talking about naval battles
and varsity crew,
their voices raspy with cigars
in underheated rooms.

Someone sewed their eyes shut
with needlepoint thread
and when they speak
they make up for it
in booming tones.

It is somewhere
out of them
alive or dead
I have sprung.
Yet not a person there seems to recognize
me.
Not one.

Bulbs

Even in the dead of winter
he is talking about bulbs.

Walking after dinner with my father.

There is snow, moonlight everywhere.
Cold. The loop is short.
We pass where he planted a hill
in the fall.
Above us stars

in the dark seed sky.
Their scattered pattern is something
we might discuss—
something he knows
from navigating boats.

I look up. It's like breathing ice.
Glitter.

My father's attention, though,
is on the knotty
wooden claws he's pressed in.
He knows where they are
below a packed layer of earth,
then all that snow above.
The tree shadows crisscross
and humps push up more sparkling white

and all he can think of,
walking with his daughter,
is bulbs.
Daffodils? I ask.
Yes, he says, this father of seven.
I planted them in clusters.

Family Dog

You left, not I.
One by one there were less of you.
Less bicycles tipping off stands.
Less leftovers I'd get of stew.
Less and less shouts and then fewer hands
To pull back my ears or smooth my head,
Or strangle my throat till my tongue went dry.
Some of you changed tastes, slept with cats instead.

Each, apart, you told me you loved me: a lie.
You each went, snapping your suitcase shut.
I loped after each car. Barking at the end
Of our drive. I could only stray so far. What
I was attached to in you would not stretch or bend.
When the last who sucked his bottle lying on my fleecy side
Left, I ambled off to where dogs bereft go
Down by the railroad tracks, and died.

New England Rock

I could never travel so far
or stay so long in the desert
or stand under veils and veils of
rain that it could change
where I began.
My life rose up this way:
a round hill studded with rocks,
a winter sea not freezing for rocking
at a rocky shore, cellars with rocks
pushing up through the floor.

I tried to get away.
I flew across the world
into a man's fig mouth. I circled
mangrove roots like a whirling drain.
I swam deranged in cocoa river mud
and huddled against palm trees waving.

The ballast in my pocket kept throwing
me down.
It was meant to steady, but it kept all of us off balance, the
    stones we carried.
It looked like slapstick. We tried to laugh it off.
The pratfalls of a drunk.
Or we had another drink
to keep it light.

Would that it were easy not to feel
so dense
in this land mined with headstones.
Would that we wouldn't turn so cold
overlooking soaked grey fields
or slapping the rope up on the bow.
You see it in people's mouths,
the granite tightening of their souls.
I move close to another for some heat
and the warmest thing I feel is doubt.

I dive into a pile of leaves
and hit the ground hard.
Would that these rocks lodged here
so fixed and stern
would give me something fixed and firm
as belief.

The Cliff Crawlers

I have to crawl up.
It is a rock-scramble crawl.
Bitten pen in my teeth.
They say it's easier if you're small,
tearing at roots till they're ragged as curtain pulls.

I slide back when I hear men
rearing motorboats out on the lumpy bay,
their engines revving out of the water, backing up,
throwing out all that man spray.

I have tried obeying and not obeying laws
and neither has taught me how to climb.
Neither and both are guidelines.
Neither and both will ever fit.
I push words around; the clouds
won't remember it.
Their shadow spreads over other cliffs
and I see someone else on a climb.
She makes it look easy, far away.
Does she claw as I claw? Is this even worthwhile
to do? It's always more full of doubt
and harder
when the climber is you.

I wouldn't mind letting go
of this hold
and standing up to see

the islands on the other side
where other women tuck and fold.
But I can only go so fast. In fact,
I'm very slow. I want things to last
longer than they do, and other slower ones
to be over soon.

I wanted a life beside him,
he handed me my coat.

Somewhere is a man who doesn't
miss me and somewhere rain
and somewhere a change waiting to sprain my life
into relief.

My hands fumble.
Clumps break into dust.
Look at the puffs of brown sailing off
like cannon shot, spreading like rust
in the sky.
The earth tilts up, pressing its belly to me.
I rub its dirty kisses from my mouth,
then kiss it again firmly.

II. LONG ISLAND

There's a man I've thought of many hours . . .

and
3
a.m.
tonight
he
sleeps
somewhere
and
though
I
no
longer
hope
to
keep
him
near
or
to
kiss
his
grave
face
or
drink
his

sigh
I
don't
mind
thinking
of
his
closed
eyes
or
of
his
mouth
parted
and
how
my
own
once
rested
there
full-hearted

Returning Monday Morning from a
Weekend on the North Fork

No night of love. In the morning a soft bandaged knock
on the guest-room door. Dreams socked in country
quiet. Radiator banging like an oil rig. A white ocean
      filling the window on the bathroom floor.

I rise somehow. Rise out of no one's padded arms.
Spit toothpaste in a cold sink. This weekend we
raked leaves. Lay in front of the fireplace.
          Had a lot to drink.

Bags in the hall in the dark. Forgetting bags.
Bags in the car. The one who drives is the one
          staying behind.

Lights on at the Corner Box. Coffee.
The newspaper I bought. Orange leaves
         on wet grey ground.

6:45. The bus door creaks. Luggage door lifts.
'Where are you getting off?' with aluminum doors
folding down and back, then the quiet interior seats.
Selection of heads, Monday morning full. Nearly
    toppling over when the bus starts to move.

I could eat tin, I'm so hungry and light.
    Could eat these words I write.

Sunday night reading in the bathtub sideways.
Kawubata Oe's son born with an open lesion
    in his brain. Later he composed music.

I sit down beside a woman in a turquoise
uniform reading Patricia Cornwell. She has
    left the window seat free.

There are many ways to live—empty, full.

The dark tar at the end of the road is still
wet from the rainy night. The sun will not
    appear today, seems like.

Do you love that, too? he said, lying
on his back. Outside it was another
    country. June. Dress in disarray.

Nothing to be done. Nothing
            I can do.

Black nets of kudzu lie thrown over
the roadside growth. Jutting up like
    collapsed roofs.

In a car an intimacy develops, he said.
How easy it was for him to slip off my
                    clothes.

The seams on the highway thwang
         beneath us like a bass.

Will you undress me? he said. *For a change.*

A house at the edge of a tipped field sits alone
in the fall morning with no one in sight under
                a bright warning sky.

The sky like white marble shoulders.

Will you undress for *me?* he said. I
held my breath. Desire breathing.
   He said, *Silence is just as good.*

The woman collecting tickets knows many
of the passengers. 'What's she majoring in?'
she says. A scarf is tied over her turtleneck.
   'You spending Thanksgiving at home?'

Will you have dinner with me tonight? he
whispered in that other land during a
cold rain. Like winter in summer. Rain
          hammering on the car.

Touching. To get close, then to break apart.
This weekend lots of touching in the kitchen.
Then breaking apart when someone comes in.
  Lots of kitchen touching all over the world.

Hot cider and rum. Leftover pie. Snapping
sticks on the lawn. Smooth stones in cold
sand. Being on a quest. Were you then?
          My turn now?

A baby in the backseat half crying.

Wishing I were a wife. Wishing I were *his* wife.
          Not that, though. Ever.

Not hardly likely. A bug smacks the windshield.
          The way he threw me down.

Traffic. The bus suddenly slows. A passenger
    returning from the bathroom staggers.

In that movie we watched, *There is only now,*
          said the dying man.

The buildings of Queens rise in the sky: a
thousand windows. Below, on the road, white
            cars glide by my resting hand.

The city noise closer like a furnace blowing,
cars leaping over the rumbling streets. I'll
see a hundred faces before I open my door.

The heart disappearing, like a road
            drying.

The Man in the Green Box

Last night he did not join me
where I waited in my bed,
but slept in a green box
close by my side, raised up,
instead.
A hand showed from a narrow slot;
the fingers short and strange
were none that I could recognize.
One knuckle had been bent, or cut.
I watched it rearrange itself
before my eyes, to grow
into the long thin shape
of hands that I well know.
I looked inside and saw
his body there, a shell.

So, tell me, I said when he woke,
why sleep away from me?
I was in shock, he said,
after my accident. You see,
I needed no distraction
if I was to get my rest,
but here—he stood—allow me . . .
And his arm with its strong breast
went round me, holding on.
We walked along a hall.
The corridor was tipped.
My face began to shake.

Don't cry, he said. I'm at your side.
I know, I said, and pressed his chest
and felt the beating thump inside.
I said, My fear
is just the slanting of this ship.
I lied.
For all night long I'd thought
this man who held me up
had died.

III. ROME

Interloper

There's a cat up on the roof
with stripes across his face.
He has the curious guarded look
of a cat who knows this place
may be inhabited
by other cats.
I see him through the window
past yellow tangles on the sill,
beyond the long pegged rack
of all my heartsick hats.
He lifts his paw and shakes off rain.
His face is wild and true.
For a moment he relieves me
of the pain of loving you.

Incantamento

I picked up the last *Tribune*
and we sped out of town.
The tall white tower squared on top
was at our back, and down I glanced
to read the news
of murders, wars, and games.
The car's gears revved, the motor hummed.
I read familiar names.

The air was white, the brownish fields
were stippled in the haze.
The Roman pines slid stately by,
the road a moving brook.
A sprinkler spat, a far-off snake,
and, dazed, I dared not move an inch
and dazed I dared not look,
fearing to break the spell
that held its yellow breath.
While he drove on. It's hard for me to say
how in the silence off of him
I saw the man and he
had not the dimmest notion
of what he meant to me.

More trees, the road grew shadowy.
Pomezia. Traffic slowed.
We could not keep up at that speed,
though I still felt the glow
of going fast while staying still.
I looked at other drivers pass.
They seemed to me all geniuses
yet none of them aware, as I was,
of the good in life,
of the stillness of his face.

And pity for the world rose up.
They were not in my place.

Sonnet on Being Touched

I stayed very still and felt his warm hand
Stroke my dark shoulder and slip down my back
And cross the horizon, wiping out lack
Of comfort which had me strapped in its band,
Leaving faint pink prints of the tourniquet's wrap
On these tired arms. I tried and could not stand.
While he—who even knows what his fingers felt—
His careful lips said not a tender word.
It changed my blood entire. Nothing I heard
Could compete with the feeling his touching dealt.
I was drugged by the singing of an unknown bird
Too powerful to stop. I feared I'd melt
And pushed him off before a deeper region stirred.
Too late. Within, it snapped, that tighter belt.

Defending Despair While Balancing on Cobblestones

He spoke
   just a peep,
 made the slightest of pleas
    not to be branded as someone
     who's scared,
    but to be more nobly seen.
 I *choose,* he said, my companion
   despair.

And where,
   she asked,
 do you go from there?
    Where will you end up
     in that endless, shoreless sea
     drifting facedown?

What's the
   difference, he asked,
 between being frightened
    and being resigned
     to constant
     despair?

It's the
   difference, she
 said, past being resigned,

between breathing air
　—as if he didn't
know—
and breathing
　water.

Mezzo Epiphany

I felt a sudden light
go off inside my head
and the grey day
which seemed so silent
stopped
as if a silent sort of bomb had dropped.
And I was in Trastevere
where you had brought me
and all at once I changed—
I was no longer fighting you.

I'd been reading about other people's lives
and was struck by how much more a life could be
than what I was living there
—terrace, tile, lemon tree—
and the striking of it
changed me.

I would have liked to believe
after all our dotted afternoons
of pulling shutters shut
and evenings taking needle
bones from fish,
after late mornings of unringing telephones
and abandoned cups of tea
that you sometimes
did love me,
but even that thought got bleached

in the white blast and it made me weep
instead of needing your great heft.
Except that you got me here.
Except that without you
I would have none of this shrapnel past
where each piece is a worthy shard.
And for a moment I almost believed in God,
but I was alone
and that was hard.

The Pale Blue Shutters

I feel the pale blue shutters
butting stone
and the nervous birds in flushing trees.
I feel the men on motorinos
sporting black glasses.
The absence of the sea.
I feel how far away you are
from me.
I feel the thin afternoon sun like a net.
The blue and white tiles
beneath my boots.
Feel you leaving again.
Feel the orange walls where you live,
the orange walls you've left.
Feel I've zero to give.
Feel the cactus by the door.
Feel the way you say good night,
pondering the floor.
Feel the tower's glinting dome.
Feel that everything's cracked apart,
and everything apart from me
is sweet.
Feel how far away I am from home
and how worn out.
Feel the Roman heat.
Feel that everything here

is yours.
Feel the ghosts of children near.
Feel them shouting out of doors.
Feel the darkness that you hold
breaking on my chest.
Feel the women you keep somewhere.
Feel left. Feel old.

IV. LONDON

Locked Out

I am further away than ever,
I am closer than ever before.
We've had a change in the weather.
Last night, locked out, I faced the door
where I'm staying
at Landsdowne Road, number 79
in W11, I'm told.
I knocked a soft knock,
then rang the bell eight times,
unable to rouse them inside
the great stony facade,
chalky, lit grey by a winter moon,
encased in scaffolding for months
to improve itself.
I contemplated climbing in,
forgetting the windows were painted shut,
and tried the ladder on the side.
I wanted to be high.
I wished I could've been on a horse in the dark
taking a long and terrible ride.
I climbed the weathered wood and thought,
This is myself at 3 A.M. climbing, a thief,
willing to smash glass, break in or flee,
thinking, This is more myself than I've been
all week,
me without a key.
I'd missed the wind blowing twenty feet above the street,
above the parked cars with white trim painted neat

around the doorways.
I was holding on to the iron bars
freezing my hands and the freezing was fine
just as the wind was fine.
I tilted and swayed.
I felt my head swoon
and suddenly stopped.
There was nowhere to go.
I was too old for this.
I knew too much.
I got back on the stoop.

After Watching a Pretty Bad Movie

Sunday. Landsdowne Road.
On the garden level waiting for lunch
I took in a series of heartrending scenes
in a Western overdone.
It really wasn't very good.
It made me feel a leanness in myself,
watching the man's long hair blow.
And my life felt faraway,
sunk back upon a kilim throw.
It made me wonder if one day
I would ever have a life that matched the one inside.
The hero of the picture made a point of being wild.
He didn't follow rules.
And all the women loved him, as his father did.
As I did, too.

There's roast chicken for lunch
and English light through leafless trees.
In me there lives an unlived self.
Sometimes she stirs.
She has a willing nature
and a recent taste for thrills.

And when the first guest leaves
after four,
an American whose accent I understand,
and people slip out baggies
rolling joints

shying away from penetrating looks
on this February afternoon
with a grey shower of rain pouring down
on the white buildings outside,
and if you are a foreigner in this town
at this in-between hour
no one will notice if you are
or are not
the real self you feel is you,
the one that wars with warring parts,
the one you feel is true.
No one will pry it from your hands
the way you pry the tangerine.
No one will turn you over
like *The Sunday Times* to see
if your next page is a revelation.

Coffee and the conversation thins.
People fold up, stir things.
They lick their joints, musing.
Suddenly it seems the light's gone dim,
and someone switches on new lights
and there's a change:
the room is newly bright and there's a yellow wall,
but you yourself are there again.

'I did not know him then.'
'I knew her well.'
'I heard things about them,
 but I shouldn't tell.'

I thought of other Sunday afternoons
when hours drifted off
in other living rooms,
of other days seen into dusk
when I might have spoken more, protected by trust.
But even then I kept a part held back.

I was not rising up.
I tried.
I willed the spirits forth
and all the time most real to me
was a man upon a horse,
a movie star, a troubled son,
an actor in a part.

Letting the Horses out of the Pen

I saw you again 3 A.M.
London taxi, torn clouds, the moon.
A long dinner glancing down a long room.
You kissed me smokily hello.
Doom in your hard face and hard eyes.
Muttering so I couldn't understand,
and somehow all that darkness
had the opposite effect.
It made me laugh.
I had a giddy feeling like the horses had been let out of the
    pen.
I thought I ought to stop
then and there
and get away
in case you caught up with me.

What a fence to lean against,
a brooding man like you.
Around you girls were twisting,
speechless.
I turned my back.
I felt you inching backwards.
Or is it what I hoped?
I knew it from afar,
the ring of a lifted latch
and the rush that comes after,
of flapping manes and kicking hooves.

Women pushed in nearby,
waiting with arched chests,
curled like wild bait.
They said, Hello there, whip me.
I like it, I do.
Take them if you want.
Here's one with big eyes,
pulling at your arm.
She says, Come on, let's go.
The dusty ground is pounding.
So go. Go, go!
I've better things to do—
horses to catch,
never mind you.

Talking of the Dead

We sat in a tall living room
and talked about the dead.

One woman there knew my friend
and spoke of his service that November day
in another high living room with views of Central Park
and yellow frigid trees.
'I was there,' she said. 'Did you attend?'

There were eulogies to recall.
'Do you do that?' a man asked. 'Speak at them all?'
And he told of how the dead do not go.
For him, they stay inside.
Someone told the story of the poet who died
on the mountain in Tibet and how they'd heard
a great booming on the set
when his plane smashed into the hills.
This reminds another of another crash,
then of a guy who lost his lung,
then of the man whose brain burst,
so he died before his son
was born.

There's one who sped into a wall,
and one who choked on gas,
and a woman with a polished cane
who didn't wait
to last it out.

One's heart is crowded through
with all of them.
One might break
or break away and stand and sway above
a vast pit of pity,
fed up, full of bitterness,
ready then to chuck it all and hurl oneself in—
'The people one loses,' the man says again,
as if to make it true,
'They stay within.'
It is another day,
in another place,
again I think of you.
And you
and you.
And
you
and you . . .

V. NEW YORK CITY

The Toast

After I've made it stumbling through the day
And liquid light surrounds the windowsill,
After paper buds have furled their wrinkled way
And, tired, I've relaxed my will,
I think of you and of your warm embrace
And recall the disturbed calmness of your face
In repose. And all the sorrow I've contained
This brilliant Tuesday in this lonely place
Vanishes. It topples down the hours strained
Till memory leaves another trace:
The time you smiled and covered me with kisses
And clicked your teeth to mine in a brisk toast
And I think, at least I have that clinking ghost.

Reception on the St. Regis Roof

Hearing you were near
I think I even felt it,
your reveling on this concrete island
without me,
greeting the women drifting by,
cloud-high and weightless
like you,
the quintessential Rooftop Guest,
hurrying away while standing still,
always somewhere else you're supposed to be,
forgetting,
and not even knowing you've forgotten,
me.
What did you notice of what floated by?
Faces shell-empty like the meringues
the flower girls feed on,
sweet and weighing air,
melting before taste
and, like you, barely there?
Your head fogged as the glass in your hand,
no doubt lacking sleep,
casually frantic to keep from being,
your old excuse, late,
too distracted to eat the food on your plate.
Did you notice the clouds banking the St. Regis roof?
Were they puffed like popcorn? Or torn?
Would you've noticed if I'd ridden by on one,
waving a pink lantern, forlorn?

While you were waltzing among chiffon
I was battling March winds down on the ground,
finding not a hint of spring,
taking every grimy detail in,
lost in the 8th Street
Saturday crowds.

Upper West Side Blizzard

Soon the snow that's falling now
at midnight this first day of spring
will melt eventually and go.
The snow, the leaves—well, everything—
brings disappearance with it.

I suppose one day I'll go to bed
and not think of how your hips
and arms
and eyes are set.
They say that it will happen soon.
I wait.
It hasn't happened yet.

The Jar

I took the man out of my jar.
I thought, That's no place for him to be.
That's no man to be in my jar.
I took him out,
and the song went out of me.
And the tree trunks hit by the rising sun
and the shape of his teeth
left.
It was for my own good that I took him out.
(After a looting, after a theft.)
He was an insult to my affections.
I took him out and
his voice was gone,
and every sound changed but one—
the beating sound kept beating on.

At first I was relieved.
I took him out and took out pain.
I thought, My jar will be ready for
a new set of teeth.
Then slowly that drained out, too:
the relief.

So there it sat, my jar on a sill
with nothing to sing about. Quiet, still.
A jar on a blank page, a jar on a roof
with nothing inside it and nothing to prove.

So I launched it. Out to sea.
A jar set adrifting, a jar on a wave.
A jar on the ocean, far from the shore.
Miraculous. Buoyant. Able to float.
But useless and empty and floating by rote.

No sound but the little tin pecks
of the waves on the glass.
My jar bobbed further and further
out to sea
till the water grew so large
and silent around it
that it was lost to me.

Waking 4 A.M.

4 A.M.
Chest split in two.
Three weeks since
put out by you.
Heart stopped.
Now in the dark
it starts again.
A dog heart waiting
for the boot,
banging *where where*
where are you

The dream that woke:
a man in a pin-striped suit
trying to seduce me.
Underwater, frozen lake.
People above us skating.
He tried to take me under the ice.
I got a fright when a creature leapt
to gnaw my foot.

I've waited without many things:
hope and rings and hope again.
Now 4:30
I wake.
The I you do not see,
the green and rooted me.

One has, after all,
needs.
Dreams know it. They remind us
what is soft.
They turn the heart,
and the turning hurts when it unlocks.

Damn you for taking my sleep,
for making me shrink like a spark
going out.
Once I put my ear
to your chest.
I swear I heard a tick.
I once even woke to the sound
of it.
Damn you for turning me hard
as a nut.

This heart for you
was playing dead.
Now, waking, 5 A.M.,
it warms. Agony of thaw.
5:30 is a surprise. Darkness

and not a sound and you not there,
but me coming into focus,
terrifyingly clear.

Beginning light
6 A.M.
First of June.
The blur into blue.
I ask myself,
Where have you *been*?
It is myself I mean.

No Conception

Nothing ever calms down,
  not with life in it.
I walk from one room to the next.
I cannot get up from the chair.
I cannot put down the drink.
I cannot stop weeping one minute,
  then I do.
Wash dishes in the sink.
I cannot speak.
Which word would come first?
I cannot think one clear thought.
I cannot rise above it. I cannot rise.
I cannot write.
I hate it, then I love it.
I cannot breathe.
I weep at the movies like a candle weeping
  on a hot night.
I cannot open the door.
I cannot take off my other shoe.
I cannot take off this face of mine
  or answer hello to anyone
  anymore.

I have nothing here except this space,
   the thing you and I might have made—
   not a place or a hole or a picture,
   but another person's soul
   who might have had your face.

Tea at Essex House

Politely telling me what's what
and who he's seen and what is new
and what new stories he's been told
and who has been involving who,
didn't say in that high room
on that same floor while sipping tea
—where he once initiated me—
what he did mention leaving,
in the elevator gloom,
hushed in eerie topaz light,
admitting a little nostalgia
as he saw me out:
that he means to stay away
and tries hard not to miss
certain silky, tree-lined days.

He returns to
his side of the sea.
We both pretend to take it lightly,
lightness being the thing he sought
when he first summoned me.
And who said one should ever
get all that one wants?
(Though it was he, actually,
inspired me
to think one could.)

And straying out through whirling doors
on Friday evening not yet late
among the cabs and high-class whores
gives tiny kisses to my face.
'Look at you,' he says.
Steps back. 'You're great,'
and tips off kilter as he turns.
And after all the lightness,
the talk of books and zipped-up coats,
he throws me one last stare
and leaves me with this heavy thing,
dense as the building's cornerstone.
I pick my way through sidewalk crowds,
and carry it off,
bearing its weight on my own.

VI. TUSCANY

Universe

The window was open to the night.
You kissed me deeply
as if you needed to get in
fast,
and even if I was slow
to catch on
I felt the sense of
what you sent
and felt how far into space
you meant to go.
Around me people shift,
becoming warm as I move away,
becoming cold,
while you—still you—
you stay still
in a way that I will
always find transporting.

Tent

In
the morning,
one of the silent
mornings when all pink
I crept out before the sun rose,
having to leave while you still slept,
I drew the bedsheet up over your long legs
and tucked it maidlike at your neck and saw
there a little tent risen up between your hips, a
peak erected that you did not see, and I
stole the image when I left, taking
the ardor I felt was mine—after
the night we'd spent—
which you still
had in your
dreams for
me.

Pulled off a Garden Wall

It was lust I had for him,
flung onto stones beneath the stars,
so when love appeared in another place,
with the giant cast of a mountain's shade,
the leafy cast of his face went dim
and became a mirage of grey and light,
still appealing with its flush, but
without the right
to enter a glowing room
where another stood up, shoved a chair,
suddenly ardent,
to keep people out.

Strange that something
rose in me
so powerfully
from being pulled off a garden wall.
Still, I made the choice
I knew was wise,
stepping through desire's hedge,
and chose love
over passion for him.

Love, I saw, was
the wider place to be.

But it was more narrow than it looked at first.
Turns out there wasn't much space

in that glowing room for me.
He slipped me in
through a crack in the door
in the crack of an hour,
between others shuffling through.
He had other people to consider
and other things to do.
And after a time
(which always tells)
when I stood at his side,
having given up stars and stones
and garden walls,
he said that though here was love
there were other things he
had to protect and save and allow to be—
and—well—
he chose those things over me.

Director

Turn me around.
Face me out the window.
Make me see
the dark green night
and the black view
and the fireflies blinking like robots
and a floating hill or two.
Make me want to live
past this moment.
I feel about to die
(I really do).
I've lost all orientation,
feel thoroughly through.
Tell me again,
Tell me what you see
with your hands on my neck.
I see the trees
with you at my back
the sky,
your stare,
the stars spilling
with you in my hair,
you pinning my arms.
Tell me again the point of the scene
and who is supposed to be telling who?
Anchor me to the chain
of you telling me
what to do.

Rabbit

No, I said. No.
So naturally you came close,
twitching your nose.
Naturally you did not go.
Later, when I was turned inside out
and my belt loops unthreaded,
after my hide was flayed,
you whispering all the while
what I took for prayer
which I now understand
was simply the flair you have
for sighing,
you took away
something I'd been clutching.
You ran off
like a rabbit,
taking my fear.
Wait! I shouted after you.
Yes, I mean! Yes!
But you were gone by then,
it being your habit
to disappear,
gone down a hole,
and despite those long ears
you couldn't hear.

The Affair

They spoke on the phone,
he with a view of the vineyards,
she in the hotel's glass stall.
What do you have on? he asked.
Her legs, in a skirt,
crossed up on the wall.
What did you do and where did you go
and what did you think
and God this is so—
and who will be at your breakfast
tomorrow?
What did you dream
and what is in store?
(They'd seen one another
an hour before.)
And how does the world
seem to you over there?
I wish you were here.
I wish this were fair.

VII. TRASTEVERE

St. Sebastian in Your Kitchen

I did not wake.
I never slept.
I left you in the dark,
asleep,
relieved of everything
while I was stark
naked on the yellow floor.
Your kitchen. 4 A.M.
I stood there with no purpose,
a wineglass, stem upended,
drying on the rack.
Some lemons lay atop some pears.
Our last cold pot of tea was there
and half a Ferrarelle, green. Me
reflected in the glass.
I toed the little spots
where yellow tiles had cracked
and pressed the tiny chips.
I did not want to think
and one moment did go blank.
A drop fell in the sink.
Then something smacked me in the face:
the blank stare of your clock.
And all at once the little hands

became a hail of darts
hitting every place you'd
ever loved in me.
And I had thought them safe,
those parts.

Collaboration

'Let us let the world in
for a moment,' he said,
and snapped the remote,
half propped up in bed.
They both were exhausted
from love and despair,
and the TV to her had
a poisonous air.

She picked up papers. Almost left the room.
But where to go?
She'd be gone soon enough.
Their work was done.

A movie came on.
He immediately knew: *'Accatone,'* he said.
On that picture he grew.
He remembered the shooting,
he remembered the crowds.
'I remember that route.'
He was laughing out loud.
He remembered exactly the street boys of Rome
and his friend the director, now long dead
and gone.

They fell under the spell of the soundtrack
whining. A funeral line came
and rounded the bend.

They watched. He remembered.
'This is close to the end.'
The streets were bleached white,
then somebody cried,
then a young man was running.
Then he got hit and died.

Later, much later,
when the room had gone dark,
he said, 'While we were watching
I had the stark thought'—he was holding
her hand, she was holding his head—
'which occurred like a blow:
how one day I'll be dead. And how
in the future there might be a time
when you'll turn on *our* movie
and I will be gone.
And you'll think the same thoughts
of all that we knew,
and beside someone else
will have the same feeling
I had beside you.'

Ducking the Paparazzi

I rode out our last hour.
Closed my eyes
on our last night.
The speckled yellow light
of the bedroom wall stayed
in my spotty view.
Till it faded. As it always does,
like a photograph not fixed,
showing weak and dim,
the way you never are,
but the way you always turn
when you go back
to being merely *him*,
no longer simply *you*.

I tear up the thing,
ripping it into two, then three,
then into four
pieces till they're so small
they can't be torn anymore.

Then comes the long blank time
(after passion)
when everything smarts.

Eventually I will begin to tick and stir.
To live, after a fashion.
One night I dance in a basement bar

and slump into a man's arms
in the lumpy back of a car.
I hear thrilling words
like fingers near my ear.
My heart begins a little flip,
a fish in an inch of water,
moving in an untrained, spastic way,
but showing signs of life, at least.
I jerk and start to turn, then am blinded by a flash.
You whom I'd put so forcefully away
appear: a flashbulb at the side of the car,
harassing me with your stare.
'Here I am,' you say as the spots go dark.
'Still there.'

Gratitude

These were the things he gave to me:
light at the end of a long hall,
a spreading ilex tree,
his hand at my elbow balancing
an unsteady walk,
the sound of fingers snapping
Queen Anne's lace. Talk.
Cobblestones beneath my feet,
crumbling yellow walls.
The feeling that I was part of history,
and terribly important,
and terribly small.

And other things he did not plan:
stumbling on a black hill in dew,
falling into canyons of men I hardly knew.
Waking in a new place
in a bright room neither of us
had seen before.
And though it was hardly his doing,
those coin-white moons.

The sound of waves is gone,
and the hills rolling off in a hot wind.
He said I never thanked him.
How does one show appreciation to breath?
What can one say, leaving?

Clasp hands, smiling?
Show that you die some?

He led me gladly.
He led me to a wide bed
and led me sadly
from it.
He told me he was trapped inside.
He handed me little pellets of belief
like stones found on a beach.

What he gave me was
different from what he said he could give.
He showed me what in him was hidden.
Bad and good.
He only half-knew what he was showing.
He only one-quarter understood.
He only one-eighth felt he was loving
and only one-sixteenth believed he could.

He shook out life like a ribbon.
It flashed where it was bent.
You can't imagine the joy it sent
through me.

Here is my gratitude.
Lament lies somewhere else.

One has every feeling when the heart appears
and I had every one for him.
Listen: no one knows the truth.
No one knows where we went.
How could they?
I never told it all.

No one will see.

Not even he
whom it might please.

Picturing What I Can Picture

One day you'll sit in the pergola's shade
and the sea will appear in another's eye
and again you'll cup the arch of a foot
and kiss the vein where the blood goes by.

Soon you will gaze in the same tipped way
at another mouth on another isle
and will follow another fluttering hem
through another hotel turnstile.

Again you'll watch a pair of calves
precede you up worn marble stairs
and will say again the things you feel
and again be taken unawares.

And soon enough you'll shift your weight
adjusting to a ruined bed,
then say you need to be alone.
And you'll give the hand a little squeeze,
and you'll pat her lightly on the head.

VIII. EN ROUTE

Say you'll always be

As dear to me
as you are now,
make me stay.
Tell me time is nothing,
that you'll never go away.
Say without me near
to you
you'd die.
Say always and forever.
My heart,
my darling,
lie.

In Flooded Atlas, Illinois

In Atlas at the crossroads
in a worm-green light
a family in tank tops
is selling peaches
Tuesday evening, late July,
from the back of a pickup truck.
A floor of water spreads
to the horizon behind
and the bags are full, despite the flood.
'We want only two,' I say,
holding out a dollar bill.
They hardly look our way,
strangers in a car the color of red pearl,
a man on a cane and a girl
with a ponytail,
just passing through this place
where houses have been swept away,
this place of sudden flat pale water day after day.

Overhead the elms drip like rotten lace.
We're parked nearby at Zeke's Café
where pink curtains ruffle the windowpanes and
we eat catfish on thick red-rimmed plates
and coleslaw and peach pie, homemade.
A choking poster is taped
to the counter's flip-top door.

Fake tulips the color of Band-Aids
sprout from narrow milky jars.
In the pages of the *Quincy Herald-Whig*
they're selling 25 lbs of rags
for flood cleanup.
Up to 5,000 pounds available, it says. *Delivery: your car.*
One feels quiet disaster
everywhere, quiet with water.

Earlier that day, driving south on 96, we hit a bird,
a sparrow.
Its feather's still stuck to the wiper
in the unstirred evening heat.
In the flat land near Hannibal
the river was silver and wide
and all that was left of the Central Illinois Expressway
was a curved twin overpass
with no road on either side,
and liquid reflecting sky
making a huge infinity sign.

'How much for just these two?'
The faces on the truck look drawn.
They've seen too much and
every sight sopped with water.
They're big, the peaches in
my hand. We don't need more,

he and I. We still have far to go
and fruit in other places to try.
And who knows how long we'll even last
on this dwindling road.
The peach sellers look through us as if we're mist.
'For only two?' they say.
'Go on.' They fold their arms and laugh,
dismissing us. We are absurd.
When we don't move right away
they wave us off,
as if we need to be reassured.

The Whisper

He said some things
the month of us.
I recall humming words.
He pointed out what irked him.
He nailed what was absurd.
He fancied a face dancing.
He heard an owl's call.
He saw the riot starting
before we noticed it at all.
He lifted me from being low
in Lira one hot night.
He told me of Lucilla
and how he held her tight.
One time he said, *I can't explain.*
One time, *I love your touch.*
But best was when he whispered,
You don't fuck me enough.

On the Road to Morogoro

On the road to Morogoro
leaving from Mikumi
we passed into the future
which did not try tomorrow,
of who was mine and who was yours
and how things ought to be.
The sky rose up a neon blue.
A moon etched there,
and Venus, too,
and you loved me and I loved you.

The Greeks said it was mad to drive
that stretch of road at night,
that bandits waited in the dark
and we might not survive.
But we were brave, or game, or brash.
Or stupid. I don't know.

An elephant went trumpeting
down into a ditch.
A truck had spilled its load
and lay abandoned on its side.
While off the road the country
grew darker than a hole.

Then we saw the lion
unmoving on the road,
dusty in the headlights.
His huge head had a powdered mane,
turning like a ghost,
as if his soul had ceased to know
the ground on which it stood.
Inside the car was hushed
with glowing dashboard lights.
You and I went creeping past.
His massive neck an arm away,
his back leg bent with grime.
He slunk along the edge.

Then I saw his hip—the gash,
a long dark lung of blood.
'He's been hit,' you said.
Your voice was soft inside the cab,
so low and close to me.
I felt it in my throat.
That's when I thought
that you were all

I'd ever need
and never would I leave you.

Can you believe I thought that?
That we would always go
roaming brave and dangerous
on wild unlit roads?

Editorial Lunch on the Ile de la Cité

'Leave the past and
look forward,' she said,
and something electric
lit up the grey.

'You were made for today
and not for the dead.'
And new ideas flooded my head,
spooning *marrons glacés.*

The Narrow Corridor

So when, I asked,
do I see you again?
Three years again till we meet?
Let me go, he said, slumped back on the wall
of the borrowed flat in the summer heat
with the one light ticking before it went black
and the sliding doors
which were tinny and cheap.
Let me go, he said, and I'll call you.
He steps by,
but I don't keep back.
I leap.
Inside, the lift is tiny
and the fake wood crazily scratched.
I'm in love with you, he says,
stricken. That's why I can't stay.
And he pushes me out.
And he leaves me with that.
Which is
everything
in its way.

On an Airplane Leaving Africa

Already I miss it   miss the *howzit?*   miss
the sound of his voice and his hands on the
wheel and the dust red smudged shirt and
the window's hissing wind   I miss his rant-
ing and our panting up the hill   I miss

   not   knowing   him   so   well
miss the intimations of hell miss his face for the
dogs and his making some tea and his smoking
too much and his standing near me miss
where we were and where we didn't go miss
already the gears shifting and how slowly we
drove on some of those roads miss the heat
and the sun and the splinters and rain and the
gulleys cracked deep and our missing the dam

   I   miss   his   teeming   brain
miss his mouth and his kiss miss his being appalled
miss him giving his spiel and the mist on the road
miss not knowing exactly what next I'd feel or exactly
how tall he was or how earnest or really how real

Through the Broken Window I
Could See Purple Jacaranda Blossoms

I'd never been
  this far away
The curtains blew
  The room was cold
The bed was filthy
  from the dogs
I felt you
  through my dusty pants
and didn't mind
  that I felt old
because I felt
  oddly home

Breathing on the Dice

I wish I were in the cold with you
in your old dirty house
with your worried eyes and blue
shirt. I wish you knew
the underneath of me,
how I keep track of everything
and try to let everything go.
I wish we'd won that game of Russian roulette
we played that week in the mountains—
or lost,
you would say,
and suffered the happy fate
of other fools who take a risk
and somehow get their way.

IX. ISLANDS

From the Window of the Shack at Shipyard Point

I have gone still,
have stilled my heart.
Let ink bleed from this tip.
I come down through the mossy woods.
I do not slip.
Though sometimes I get dizzy looking up.
Sometimes I have rapture in the fog,
and sometimes simply disappear,
transfixed by the wrinkled sea.

Alone's the only way to here.

Only after days and days
do I remember
you must leave behind
the phone and key.

Something goes by in the little waves,
a prow having sunk,
washed in from the bay.
It has a sharp point,
drifting by, passing me.

I wonder if it's good
or just strange
to believe that by scratching

with this little point
I might move or
change anything.

All of it's been said before,

but just as true as nothing's changed,
the world's not been as it is now.
Never was another time
the instant that I make this rhyme
the same.

But it should not go unremarked
—a contradiction understood—
that in the urge to give some joy
or stanch some pain by telling tales
of what we've found and what we do
that it is done by one who must
sit in silence,
dream and brood
alone, half lost,
in some dark wood.

After Labor Day

The light is spiking off the water
in slivered grey spears.
I've been here for months.
Seems like years.
Worshiping the crying birds,
the rusted pen and warped desk,
the seaweed spreading like women's hair
over the rocks,
the light sea and the dark trees.

After work
I worship the light more.

In the silver crosses
slicing the waves I'm struck
as one is by autumn's brightness
of all the passion one contains
and despair to think
from this spruce shore
how I will never show it.
Or even the smallest part
of what rises in me

in a certain particular way.

I will never even come close
to the height of the sky today.

I think of the milky spark in
my aunt's blue eye
as she relates some delight
or of the way her husband says
he seeks redemption
and worries he will die
before he gets out of his yellow
clouded place.

I don't forget how one man held me
one whole long night
not letting go,
checking my face now and then
for any signs
as the dirt road outside went from rust to rose.

I am under a hat. I am in the sun.
I hold this pen and stop.

That light on the sea.
I could explode.
I have a monster urge to feel
the smooth side

of his flank again.
Or something live and warm.
Or even something
sharp and cold.

I am too moved.
I've turned deranged,
practicing restraint for work's sake.

It's one way to arrange a life.

I think my life must change.

On Hog Island

The ends of the tall grass rose
past his chin and nose
and beyond that the sky
was glowing pink
along the dead blue hills.

Summer just gone.
The crushed smell of something between
spruce and snow.
He said, I had misgivings, you know.
He said it with his straight blue eyes.
But this, he said, is not less.
This, he said, is more.

And he qualified it
with an admission
so precious to the old,
or at least to one who has
a few years folded beneath her.
He pulled me up
with an extra tug
the way we'd hauled the boat over the flat rocks
to leave it untied on the rocky shore.
Fixing me in his gaze,
he said,
That's never happened to me
before.

Dawn in a Chilmark Barn

6 A.M.
this morning
the trees out the barn window
were golden, blurry and lit.
When I put on
my glasses I saw
it was the sun
like Africa.

In my dream
I'd been driving
through a Swiss town, but Italian, too,
but mainly Beverly Farms. Mum
was a bag lady in the passenger seat.
My sister in the back
with a boy. They were explaining why
another woman was more beautiful
than I. My father, as always, was driving.
Suddenly he stopped and got out,
wearing his parka with the fur hood.
His eyes were blue—his eyes are brown—
and the whites very white.
I have to go,
he announced.
He looked like other men I know.
His mouth was pursed,
fearful.

Please don't, I said.
For once telling him how
I felt. Please. Shaking.
Please stay.
I'm sorry, he said, stricken eyes, nothing to do.
No, I sobbed. No! Just this once
I'm asking you.
Please *please* don't go.
He turned. I have to.

I woke and saw the eaves
of the little barn.
Yellow trees lit with sunrise, dead
roses in the corner. Rust.
Smooth rocks in piles
from the beach. Awake
I saw the truth of it: no one stays.
My backbone seemed to crack.

In the thin morning air I saw
clearly
what thickens through the day
—otherwise it's too much to bear—
that it only ends this way.

A NOTE ABOUT THE AUTHOR

Susan Minot grew up in Manchester-by-the-Sea, Massachusetts. Her first novel, *Monkeys*, was published in a dozen countries and received the Prix Femina Étranger in France. She is the author of *Evening, Folly, Lust & Other Stories,* and most recently the novella *Rapture.* She wrote the screenplay for Bernardo Bertolucci's *Stealing Beauty.* She currently lives on North Haven Island in Maine.